婆婆和葫蘆瓜

一個印度的民間故事

Buri and the Marrow

An Indian Folk Tale

Retold by Henriette Barkow
Illustrated by Lizzie Finlay

Chinese translation by Sylvia Denham

mantra

從前有一個老婦人，她與她的兩隻狗一起住，拉路和巴路。
她唯一的女兒住在森林很遠的另一邊。

Once, there was an old woman who lived with her two dogs, Lalu and Bhalu.
Her only daughter lived on the other side of a forest, far away.

有一天，她對她的狗說：「這是探訪我女兒的時候了，留在這裡等我回來。」她執拾行裝後便起程去了。

One day, she told her dogs, "It's time for me to visit my daughter. Stay here until I return." She packed her bag and went on her way.

她還未走到森林深處便遇到一隻狐狸。
「婆婆，婆婆，我想吃你，」牠咆哮著說。

She hadn't gone far into the forest when she met a fox.
"Buri Buri, I want to eat you," he snarled.

「啊，狐狸，你不能吃一個像我這樣瘦的老婆婆，
等我從我的女兒處回來，那時我會又肥又好吃。」
「婆婆，你回來時，我便會吃你，」狐狸咆哮地說。

"Oh fox, you don't want to eat a thin Buri like me. Wait until
I return from my daughter's, then I'll be nice and fat."
"Buri Buri, when you return, I shall eat you," snarled the fox.

老婦人繼續她的旅程，直至她遇到一隻老虎。
「婆婆，婆婆，我想吃你，」牠怒吼著說。

The old woman continued her journey until she met a tiger.
"Buri Buri, I want to eat you," he growled.

「啊，老虎，你不能吃一個像我這樣瘦的老婆婆，
等我從我的女兒處回來，那時我會又肥又好吃。」
「婆婆，你回來時，我便會吃你，」老虎怒吼地說。

"Oh tiger, you don't want to eat a thin Buri like me. Wait until
I return from my daughter's, then I'll be nice and fat."
"Buri Buri, when you return, I shall eat you," growled the tiger.

老婦人又繼續她的旅程，直至她遇到一隻獅子。
「婆婆，婆婆，我想吃你，」牠吼叫著說。

The old woman went on her way again until she met a lion.
"Buri Buri, I want to eat you," he roared.

「啊，獅子，你不能吃一個像我這樣瘦的老婆婆，
等我從我的女兒處回來，那時我會又肥又好吃。」
「婆婆，你回來時，我便會吃你，」獅子吼叫地說。

"Oh lion, you don't want to eat a thin Buri like me. Wait until
I return from my daughter's, then I'll be nice and fat."
"Buri Buri, when you return, I shall eat you," roared the lion.

最後，老婦人終於抵達她的女兒的家。
「啊，女兒呀，我的旅程真可怕，首先我遇到一隻狐狸，跟著便是一隻老虎，之後又有一隻獅子，牠們都等著吃我。」

At last, the old woman arrived at her daughter's house.
"Oh Daughter, what a terrible journey I've had. First I met a fox, and then a tiger and then a lion. They're all waiting to eat me."

「不要擔心，媽媽，我們會想辦法解決的，
但現在你必須先休息和吃一些東西，」
她的女兒說。

"Don't worry Mother, we'll think of something. But first,
you must rest and have some food," answered her daughter.

老婦人在女兒的家住了三個月，在這段期間，
她吃了很多東西，變得又肥又胖。

The old woman stayed with her daughter for three months. During that time, she was given so much to eat that she became nice and fat and round.

當回家的時候到了，老婦人問她的女兒：
「我應該怎樣做呢？所有的動物都等著吃我。」

When it was time to go home, the old woman asked her daughter,
"What shall I do? All the animals are waiting to eat me."

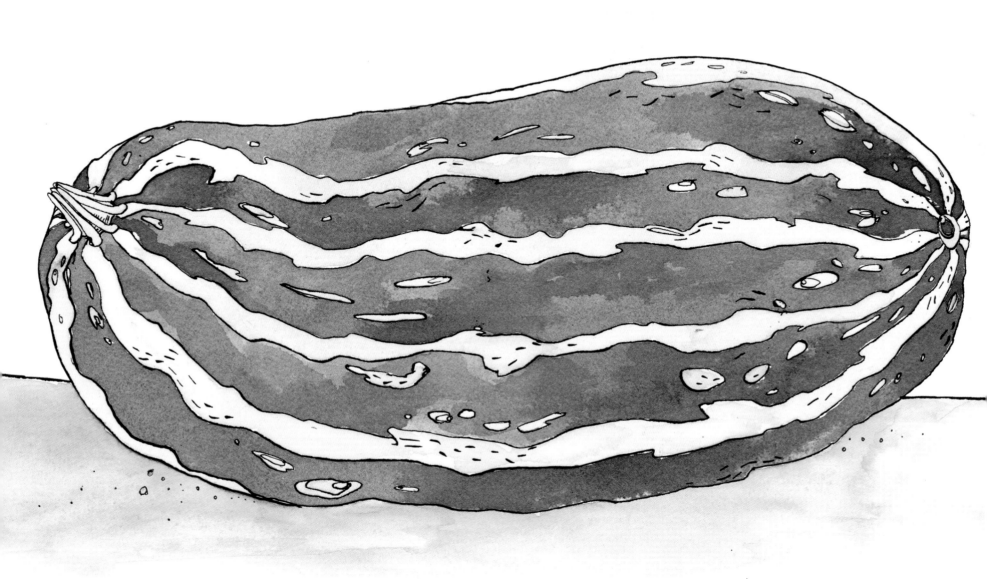

「來，媽媽，我有一個計劃，」女兒一邊答，一邊走到花園去。
她在那裏摘了最大的一個葫蘆瓜，把頂部切去，再挖空瓜瓤。

"Come Mother, I have a plan," answered the daughter, and went into the garden.
There, she picked the largest marrow she could find, cut off the top and hollowed it out.

「爬進去，然後我推動葫蘆瓜，它便會轉到你的家。再見，媽媽。」
「再見，女兒，」老婦人擁著女兒說。

"Climb in. Then, I'll push the marrow, and it will roll you home. Goodbye Mother."
"Goodbye Daughter," answered the old woman, as they hugged each other.

女兒把葫蘆瓜的頂部封蓋好，然後將它一推。
當葫蘆瓜沿著路轉動時，婆婆細聲地唱：
　　「大瓜轉又轉，
　　我們往家轉。」

The daughter sealed the marrow and gave it a push.
As it rolled along, Buri quietly sang:
　　"Marrow turning round and round
　　We are rolling homeward bound."

當它轉到獅子時，牠怒吼道：「葫蘆瓜，你又大又多汁，
不過我正在等我的婆婆呢。」於是牠將瓜一推。
當葫蘆瓜轉動時，婆婆唱著：
　　「大瓜轉又轉，
　　　我們往家轉。」

When it reached the lion, he roared, "Marrow you're big and juicy,
but I'm waiting for my Buri," and he gave it a push.
As it rolled along, Buri sang:
　　"Marrow turning round and round
　　We are rolling homeward bound."

當它轉到老虎時，牠怒吼道：「葫蘆瓜，你又大又多汁，
不過我正在等我的婆婆呢。」於是牠將瓜一推。
當葫蘆瓜轉動時，婆婆唱著：
「大瓜轉又轉，
我們往家轉。」

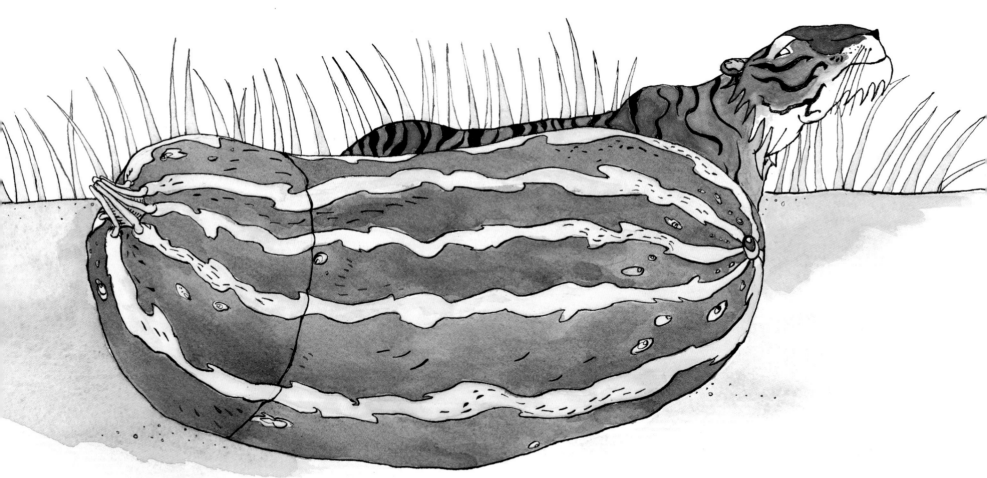

When it reached the tiger, he growled, "Marrow you're big and juicy,
but I'm waiting for my Buri," and he gave it a push.
As it rolled along, Buri sang:
"Marrow turning round and round
We are rolling homeward bound."

當它轉到狐狸時，牠看著葫蘆瓜咆哮地說：
「葫蘆瓜，你又大又多汁，但我知道你收藏著我的婆婆呢。」

But when it reached the fox, he looked at it and snarled,
"Marrow you're big and juicy, but I know you're hiding my Buri."

狐狸猛然撲向葫蘆瓜，將它撕開，看到裏面的老婦人。
「婆婆，婆婆，我現在要吃你了，」牠咆哮著說。

And the fox pounced onto the marrow and tore it apart. Inside, he found the old woman.
"Buri Buri, I'm going to eat you now," he snarled.

「啊，狐狸，你吃我之前，請讓我再看看我的家，」老婦人懇求道。
「婆婆，婆婆，我會讓你看你的家的，」狐狸說。

"Oh fox, before you eat me, please let me see
my home again," pleaded the old woman.
"Buri Buri, I WILL let you see your home,"
said the fox.

當他們抵達老婦人的屋子時，她大聲叫道：
「拉路！巴路！救我！救我！」
兩隻狗跑出來，追著狐狸，牠走呀，走呀，
直至牠逃脫了。

When they reached the old woman's house, she screamed,
"Lalu! Bhalu! Save me! Save me!"
The two big dogs raced out of the house and chased the fox,
who ran and ran until he got away.

當牠停下來時，牠嘆息道：「婆婆，婆婆，
你勝過我，現在我只有葫蘆瓜做晚餐。」
至於那老婦人，她再也沒有被狐狸煩擾了。

When he stopped, he sighed, "Buri Buri, you got the better of me.
Now, all I have is marrow for my tea."
As for the old woman, she was never troubled by the fox again.

For
Chabi Dutta whose telling of the story inspired this book.
H.B.

For
my mum and dad, with love.
L.F.

Buri and the Marrow is a Bengali folk tale. The word *Buri* means *old woman* in Bengali

Mantra Lingua
Global House, 303 Ballards Lane, London N12 8NP
www.mantralingua.com

First published in 2000 by Mantra Lingua
This edition 2006
Text copyright © 2000 Henriette Barkow
Dual Language Text copyright © 2000 Mantra Lingua
Illustrations copyright © 2000 Lizzie Finlay

A CIP record for this book is available from the British Library